# WHEN THE

# Healing

# BEGINS

a book of poetry from the depths of my heart

Tangila Roberson

# Acknowledgements

When I closed my eyes, I could see that the journey was not going to be easy, but the path was very clear. Thank you to those who helped light the path along the way. Thank you to those who talked things over, read, offered comments, supported, and encouraged me.

Thank you to my parents, James and Gertrude, for always supporting the path I've chosen and trusting that I was going in the right direction. I love you both more than any words could ever say.

Thanks to Rachel Bishop who conquered the challenge of editing a poetry book.

A special thanks to Ashlee Henry for making this all come together and making sure I had an amazing cover. I could not have done this without you.

# Introduction

*When the Healing Begins: A Book of Poetry from the Depths of My Heart* is a collection of poetry and life experiences that speaks of love in its array of colors through the eyes of a young and impressionable mind. In it, I've shared stories that have inspired a lot of my poetry and shaped my view of love. I started writing poetry at the age of thirteen, and even at such a young age, my writings were all about being loved, not feeling loved or wanting to be in love. As I reflect back on my poetry, I get the sense that I wrote out my love life before I actually lived it, unknowingly so. This book expresses the inner thoughts tucked away in my heart as I grew and matured, all which experiencing love in its many different forms.

I wasn't able to voice my thoughts, as I was very shy and reserved, so I took to pen and paper to be my voice when it came to the matters of the heart. I could see love all around me, but exemplified in many different ways that I didn't quite understand. I viewed love as more emotional than something tangible. If someone gives you something as a sign or token of their love, then they take it back, is it still love? If I no longer have this symbolism of love and it no longer belongs to me, can I still call it love?

In my early twenties, I was given the name Ice Princess by a potential suitor. He said I was so loveable and beautiful, but my heart was cold as ice. I didn't really get it then, but as I later came to know myself a little better, I realized my heart had been broken too many times by those closest to me. As a result, I learned to cope and I became very guarded and protective of my heart in an attempt to shield it from others hurting it. It has taken years to get to a place of healing where I can really allow myself to trust again and allow myself to love and be loved. That has inspired what is to come as you read this book. Through my poetry, I share my life, my wounds, but most of all I share my heart.

As I journeyed through life, there were highs and lows of being in love, losing love, being deceived by love, but also the happiness of love. My realization is that love, for some people, is tangible, but for me genuine love always flows from the depths of a person's heart. Whatever you hold dear to your heart is truly what you love. "For where your treasure is, there your heart will be also." Matthew 6:21 (KJV)

**How do you know when the healing begins? When the hurt goes deeper than the eyes can see, and you just want the pain to go away. When you find yourself just coping and not dealing with the real cause of your hurt, that's when it's time for the healing to begin.**

I want to help guide you in exposing the hidden pain that can go undetected, leaving emotional wounds that never seem to heal. I want to challenge you to dig deep into the root cause of every hurt and pain that seems to always show up and send you spiraling back to your past and allowing it to hinder your future.

*When the Healing Begins* is a book that allows you to examine yourself by first identifying the problem. Once you can identify the problem, you then can begin to target that area of your life and allow the healing process to begin. I will share with you personal experiences that created emotional wounds throughout my life. But I also will share with you how I was able to move forward in the healing process.

There were various accounts that took place in my life that resulted in unhealed emotional wounds and the effects of those wounds. No matter your age, sex, or race, this book is sure to jump-start your journey to a life of liberty. So when does this healing process begin? **Right now!**

Hurt can come from many different places, but when left untreated, it can create deep wounds within us. When we don't allow ourselves to totally heal from our past, it can cause us to keep looking back, and never move forward to our purpose in life.

Countless people experience hurt in different areas of their lives. By allowing hurt to take root within us, we allow it to create unforgiveness, bitterness, resentment, and strife that are often hidden within that we may not recognize. When we fail to search our hearts, it gives room for them to stay hidden within us while it openly destroys us. If you will search within your heart and identify what is really hurting you, you will discover an inner peace longing to replace the hurt.

The deepest pain I can unearth is from death, and having to say goodbye. After years of living with emotional wounds, I met someone that catapulted my healing process. God sent me an angel and she saw beyond what the eyes could see and saw how delicate and fragile I had become. She encouraged me, prayed for me, and she protected me from those who pretended to be there to lift me up, but all the while they were trying to tear me down.
She showed me how to walk in humility and how to forgive others through my pain. She introduced me to her world of ups and downs, highs and lows, but also to triumph and victory. I owed her so much more than I could ever give, but for all that she gave me, I was able to give her a portion of it back when she really needed it most.

The hardest thing I ever had to do in my life was to watch her gradually make her transition from this world. The last month I spent with her, I held on to each day because they all meant so much, knowing that I wouldn't have many more. Those days were some of the toughest days I've ever had to live. Through it all came my hurt, my wounds, but then my joy.

# Take My Hand

"Take my hand and follow me," the angel said.
It was time for you to leave, and from this earth to be led.

But it just seems as though we couldn't let go, the pain was too much to bear.
Now the thought of you bring tears to my eyes, so many things we'll never
get to share.

That time has come to say our goodbyes and to let you take your rest.
No sadness, no worries, only a peace of mind for God knows what is best.

"Take my hand and follow me," the angel said;
In our hearts you'll always be, but from this earth you were led.

# Goodbye for Now My Friend

So long, now you are gone, never to return again, goodbye for now my friend. A beating heart full of pain, memories of what we shared embedded in my brain. Gone today and no tomorrow, days short and nights are so long. These teary eyes of mine just won't seem to close.

No longer able to express one's inner thoughts, no longer able to be a part of your heart. It was so hard to let go and even harder to go on, but from the life on this side you have transitioned beyond.

I must wipe away these tears and let go of all my fears. Awaking each day, knowing that you will always be in my heart, even though the day has come that we will forever be apart. You were laughter, you were smiles, you were a part of me, but no more you will I get to see.

Your presence brought sunshine but your death brought us pain, everyday is cloudy with 100% chance of rain. So long, now you are gone and never to return again. Goodbye for now, my friend.

## Painting the Picture...

When I was a child, I remember falling off my bicycle and scraping my knees or cutting my heel when my foot would slip off of the pedals. There were many bumps and bruises from falls and rough playing throughout my childhood. There was one particular time when I fell off my bike and the gravel scraped my left knee pretty bad. It started to bleed and the blood rolled down my leg as I limped and hobbled into the house for my mom to make it all better. Just like a mother, she cleaned and bandaged it and sent me on my way.

As time goes by, we know physical wounds eventually heal, but this one hung around for a while. I remember this one so vividly because it took a really long time to heal. I would bump into something, or scrape it against my pants as I put them on and every time this happened, it caused it to bleed and hurt all over again. I would get so frustrated at myself because it seemed as though my knee would never heal. Finally, the scab began to take form. I was thrilled because, even at that age, I knew that a scab meant healing was in full effect. It won't be long now, I thought.

Then it happened. I was with my parents, we were leaving from this store and as we approached the exit, it was pouring down rain. Because we didn't have an umbrella, my dad went to pull the car to the front entrance so we wouldn't get soaked getting into the car. My dad opened the driver side door and pushed the front seat up. As I made my mad dash through the rain, would you believe that I hit my knee again? No, not the good knee but The Knee! Yes, it broke through my scab, yes, it began to bleed, and yes, I began to cry. I think I cried more not because of the pain, but because I was tired of this knee getting in my way.

Just like the scab on my knee had to come into play as part of the healing process, the same thing has to take place in our personal lives. When we get hurt from emotional cuts and bruises, we have to go through the same process before the healing actually takes place. We can be hurt by family members, people we are in relationship with, misbehaving children, people we go to church with, people on our job, the death of a loved one, financial set back, failed marriages, decline in our health, and the list goes on.

When the healing process is halted or in some cases never begins, we do what we do best – just ignore it instead of actually preparing it for healing. If you have a sore, you would put ointments and use bandages to aid the healing. However, if you keep picking at the sore and pulling the scab off, it takes longer to heal, risking infections, and often times leaving behind scars. As for my knee, it did eventually heal, but there is a permanent scar that is there to remind me of that fall from my bike. This scar doesn't hurt, and it has healed completely; often times it's not even thought of, but I am still reminded of how it came to be. Even when time has gone by and it's not even a thought in my mind, someone else sees the scar and asks, "What happened to your knee?" and just like that I instantly remember the long recovery of my knee.

Now I have no emotional scars from this knee story, but I'm trying to paint a picture of how this works in our day-to-day lives when we carry around unhealed emotions from our past. We have to be careful not to just suppress our feeling and allow them to internalize, all the while creating those hidden emotions, the ones that live in our hearts tucked away.

I want to paint a picture so vivid that you see it in its entirety and not in pieces. When we see the picture as a whole, we understand it more and can process it better. Our life is like a giant puzzle, and as we go through life, we continuously add pieces to the puzzle, making it one big picture. How much time it takes depends on how well we adjust, regroup, and move forward when trials and tribulations come. I want to show you how to move beyond the sores, the wounds, and the scars, while allowing the healing process to take shape in your life.

It is my hope that as you read through this book, you will be able to take my journey as a motivator to push forward into greater life expectancies. This is where you start to be honest with yourself about everything that you are aware of that is hurting you and possibly hindering you. It's time to stop using our hurt as a defense mechanism out of fear of losing control of something that actually has control over us.

Treating the symptoms and not the cause only keeps us guessing and fixing other people and not our self. We lose valuable time and prolong the process dealing with issues that are not really the problem. Don't get side tracked and busy fixing things that are not really broken.

# I Am

You say that you want to know who I am.

I am what you see, standing tall and proud; oh yeah, that would be me.

I am a woman. I am sincere. I don't listen to everything that is whispered into

my ear.

So you want to know who I am. So I tell you that I'm beautiful, smart, kind,

and sweet.

I am exactly who stands before, I am just what you see.

So you say you want to know who I am. So I tell you I am a voice, I am a cry

in the night.

I am a smile on your face, I am just right.

So you still don't know who I am?

I am a heart full of love that stretches far and wide for everyone to see.

I am being me.

# When I Closed My Eyes

The pain in my heart was buried too deep for you to see.

That is why it was my little secret that I chose to keep.

The mysteries of my heart, how beautiful they were when masked and in disguise.

I pulled back the mask and the true beauty I saw when I closed my eyes.

Everybody wants happiness, nobody wants the pain, but you can't see the rainbow until you've had some rain.

So often, we seek guidance, counseling, and advice for healing, but we miss the key factor. We have not identified or acknowledge the areas in our lives that truly need healing. We have to dig deep, and for some, the digging will be deeper than for others. The objective is to get to the root cause of the problem and uproot it. We have to go beyond the surface in order to find out why certain past events continue to plague our lives.

When you begin to bring past events to the surface, it will require you to go back and search for answers. Remember that you are not going back to stay, but to only get what you need to release those feelings that keep you from moving forward. You may realize that some of the things you thought you had gotten over were actually suppressed, or as we say, "Swept under the rug." Because we never deal with these issues, little things will trigger emotions and set us off at the unlikeliest times. You may even find yourself enraged and lashing out at others over the smallest things for no apparent rhyme or reason. Don't try to rush the process, but allow for time to shape and mold you into the man or woman that you are striving to be. You have to be patient and steadfast in knowing that your end will be better than your beginning.

My digging came after many years of just coping and internalizing all of my hurt and pain. Just when I thought I had dug far enough, I had to dig a little deeper. I discovered that a lot of my hurt was caused by things that happened very early on in life. I also realized that wounds that I thought were healed were very much still exposed and either partially scabbed or not at all in the healing process. There were even some wounds that I had suppressed for many years that weren't discovered until they resurfaced as an adult. It's time to stand in the mirror and get to know the person staring back at you. I had to face that image and accept the person who was looking back at me. I'd come to realize that this tough outer exterior was not who I was, but the person I had become in order to cope with what I was feeling emotionally. As a result, I trod very lightly when it came to sharing personal things about me to others.

As I looked back over my life, I can say that I had the "just get over it" or "suck it up" attitude. There was an emotional disconnect when it came to seeing life through the eyes of others. I developed trust issues and kept feelings that were deep inside to myself. I totally suppressed my feelings and internalized my pain. Meanwhile, my mind created a barrier that kept others at a distance so I wouldn't be hurt again.

As you read further, you will find that hurt doesn't discriminate, and it can take root at any time or place in your life. After a while, I just told myself that it was just the way I was. I had the perfect defense against not getting hurt by people. The game plan was I wouldn't bother them and therefore they wouldn't bother me. Funny, but this was my approach to life for many years.

Can you imagine trying to live in a world all by yourself? It's get very lonely, very quickly.

After I began to identify things like unforgiveness, anger, and resentment, I didn't like that person and I wanted to be free from that bondage. The only thing I was missing was that key factor that I stated at the beginning – the root cause. I would eventually come into the knowledge that a lot of crippling situations that happened in my life were of my own disobedience, and some were the result of other people. It wasn't until that point in my life that I could begin the healing process. I first had to start with emptying myself and getting rid of all of the junk that I held on to throughout the years.

As I began to dig, I got to a dark place and I realized that I had harbored the feeling of being rejected from a very early age in life. Not the rejection you may be thinking of, such as rejection from a guy that I really admired. No, this rejection was from someone close to me, someone who I wanted nothing more than to accept me and to treat me with the same care and compassion that others got. I can vividly remember childhood events as early as four or five years old. I was able to identify that something was not right, and I didn't like the way it made me feel. So, being too young to understand it all, I grew up suppressing my feelings. I became insecure about who I was and how I looked through the eyes of others. These were my secret thoughts that kept me hiding from the world and never really showing people who I was on the inside or what I could be. I had the fear of failing and not measuring up to what I believed other people's expectations of me were.

The first act that negatively affected my life was rejection from my maternal grandmother. Every child wants to be special in the eyes of their grandparents, but I wasn't and I couldn't understand why. I truly believed that I was loved, but emotionally I struggled with understanding their way of being loving grandparents. I distinctively remember feeling that my maternal grandmother loved me, but she showed it differently. I wanted her to treat me the same as she treated my brother and the other grandchildren but it just didn't happen. I can recall birthdays, even Christmas, and everyone would have something from her except for me. There were many excuses over the years, but I never believed them, but I accepted them to shield my emotions. I wanted to believe that she miscounted the number of children, or that she couldn't remember my size. I wanted to believe that her leaving me out was not intentional, but I would learn some years later that it was. I struggled to have much of any kind of relationship with any of my grandparents. Either they were just not there or didn't put forth much of an effort to build the relationship.

The feeling of being rejected and not being good enough and loved weighed heavy. I began to become this very emotional child whose feelings were very easily hurt. I became known as "water bucket" and "cry baby" by my brother and cousins who I grew up alongside. They didn't know how it made me feel being children themselves, but I believe that they sensed something was not right. I will never forget that every time my grandmother excluded me from the treats and goodies, my brother and my cousins would all share theirs with me. Looking back and seeing that I actually would end up with more after they all shared with me. Nevertheless, it did not change the fact that I had wounds that would take some twenty plus years to heal.

At about age twelve or thirteen, after harboring my feelings for years, never telling anyone how I felt, I wanted some answers. I wanted to know why? Why did I get treated differently from the others? I needed to know what had I done to make my grandmother treat me this way. So one evening while she was cooking, I walk up to her very calmly and asked, "Why do you treat me different from the rest of them?" She instantly knew what I was talking about, and her demeanor quickly changed. She stopped dead in her tracks and looked at me with this look of disbelief, as if to ask how I would dare ask such a thing. I didn't have to say another word before she responded. She said in a very stern and aggressive tone, "Tangie, you have a daddy that will do for you and the rest of them don't." Just as quickly as she acknowledged me, in the same like manner she dismissed me and turned away and continued to cook.

I slowly turned and walked out of the kitchen and went to my room to cry. I remember thinking, "What does that mean?" Was I really supposed to understand her justification? Was her answer really supposed to make all the hurt and now this anger just go away? Needless to say, I never asked her again, nor did she change how she treated me. It was at that pivotal point in my life that I realized that was how it was going to be, so I better adjust quickly. It was then that the "cry baby" died and the Ice Princess began to surface.

Often times our biggest setback is unforgiveness. We hold on to unforgiveness because it validates us to feel the way we do in our hearts.

It justifies our actions or lack thereof. We have someone or something to blame for how we feel and/or act, but the truth is that we are not accepting responsibility for our actions and pushing blame to others to free us from any accountability.

But how many of you know that my wounds only grew bigger and deeper as time went on. Some years later at the age of sixteen, my grandmother unexpectedly passed away. I was saddened by her death, but I was still hurt, angry, and full of unforgiveness, and I carried this hurt into my adulthood. It changed who I was as a person and it shaped me into who I'd become. The reality of it was that even though she couldn't physically create any more hurt in my life, the damage was already done. Anyone who ever did anything to hurt me in the least way, I held on to it and it was secretively destroying me because I would not let it go. I never talked about it; I just kept right on living. High school came and went, so did college, graduate school, jobs, and relationships, but the one thing that seemed to hang around was my ability to keep my hurt and pain bottled up inside.

I share this with you to show how something you may never give much thought to may actually be the one thing that needs the most attention. It wasn't until I was in my mid-to-late twenties that I realized that I had not forgiven my grandmother as well as other people that hurt me. Suppressing our feelings can keep us from the truth and keep us bound to a hurtful and painful past.

I know that everybody's story is not the same and people have different life experiences, but we may share the misfortune of being bound by our past. I do believe that my grandmother, as well as my other grandparents genuinely loved me, but they all showed it in ways that I didn't quite understand. I am no longer that hurt little girl seeking to be loved; instead I just love expecting nothing in return.

# A Grandparent's Love

The love of a grandmother, what a pleasure it must be. Some things may never be known because you really didn't get to know me.

The love of a grandfather, oh it must have been such fun. I couldn't tell you, maybe if I wasn't a granddaughter and instead had been a grandson.

The thoughts of a kid wanting a grandparent's love, seems as though I'm always disappointed because I never got what this kid called "love."

So now I write my grandparents this poem, but I'm no longer offended because I have the strength to carry on.

If I could go back in time and tell you what was on my mind, I would have simply asked just for us to spend a little quality time.

Even though I didn't say much, I was only being me, but I would have loved something simple like getting a gift from you under the Christmas tree.

I never asked for a lot – actually I never asked for anything. Was it too much for you to have at least remembered my name?

The love of a grandmother from the eyes of a child; did you ever wonder how it made me feel when you repeatedly left out?

So many emotions, I just could never really explain why an adult would inflict on a child so much emotional pain.

There were so many birthdays and holidays that came, always an excuse why none of your gifts display my name.

The love of a grandfather, absent to say the least, I met you once and then you died, leaving no memories of you and me.

The love of my grandparents, what a pleasure it must be. Some things may never be known because they really didn't get to know me.

# Those Words

I know what I heard but that's not really what you said, but as time goes by these negative words keep playing in my head. Were they meant to hurt me? It's kind of hard for me to tell, but if you look into my eyes, you can see the path of my tears that fell.

Were they to cut deep into my soul? Piercing into my heart to be emotionally scolded? But there is no blood and where are my wounds? They are hidden inside because I haven't figured out what I should do.

If you had to say those words over again maybe you wouldn't choose to do so. I think it's time for me to move on and just let all of this hurt go. I'm more than those hurtful words, and I'm stronger than ever before. Time heals all wounds so I no longer want to even the score.

Now is the time to forgive those that hurt me and to dry all those weeping tears from my eyes. Although, there still may be days that I remember the hurt and want to just get mad and cry.

I'm letting it all go and I won't keep it bottled up inside. God has given me a

powerful voice and I speak and I say today is the day my soul will rise.
It will rise above criticism, above all negative thoughts. It will rise above my deepest and darkest secrets and my silent thoughts. It makes me free to love and free to smile from within, no more of your hurtful words will I let enter in.

I know what I heard but that's not really what you said, but as time goes by I no longer will let those negative words keep playing in my head.

# Invisible

Do you see what I see? Can you feel what I feel? To be invisible in this make-believe world of shallow thrills.

Hey let's talk and share a few laughs, tell me more of this invisible world that I can't see although I'm looking at it through shatterproof glass.

So long are the days of searching for a reason to be. So lonely are the nights spent with no one there but just me.

I have to figure this one out, so much time has passed. I'm having a sense of urgency to break through this shatterproof glass.

I need to rally the troops and assemble the team. Get them all into position to take down an enemy that cannot be seen.

The war has started but yet to be won because the battle that lies within my heart has just now begun.

Open up these blind eyes, behold I can see, that the invisible world has always been staring right back at me.

Invisible I said, but clearly I see. The masquerade of this life that has been desperately and patiently waiting for me.

Do you see what I see? Can you feel what I feel? To be invisible in this make-believe world of shallow thrills.

# A Letter To A Friend....

If you were still here, I'm sure we'd still be the best of friends, but life happens and what our future would have held, I'll never know. Sixteen years seems like such a long time ago, but often I think of you and memories start to flow through my mind. You once asked, "Can you stand the rain? Because there will be stormy weather." I didn't give it that much thought because I didn't know that the stormy weather was just around the corner.

No one would have ever guessed that your life would be taken in such a tragic way. I, for one, could not have imagined the events that took you away and dealing with the unknown keeps questions running through my head. So I write you this letter and after sixteen years, I share my heart all over again. There would be times when I didn't have the words to say, but you knew me well enough and filled in the blanks. You knew just what would put a smile on my face, and I loved how you made it a point to create those special moments just for me. I remember those early morning wake up calls at 6:30 A.M. and hearing your voice on the other end saying, "Good morning, Tangie." I remember those mornings that you would walk to my house just so you could see me off for the day. It was the little things you did that would always put a smile on my face and those little things are what keep you tucked safe and secure in my heart even today.

Time does seem to heal all wounds, but also knowing that you were such a caring and loving person and the memories that you left behind made the healing process easier. Although we were both young and feeling our way around this thing called love, I knew that I occupied your heart and to know I had a place there was the greatest memory you could have ever given me. So I say thank you for showing me that love went beyond material possessions or giving of gifts. You showed me that when you love someone, you invest in that relationship to make it invaluable, worth more and more as time continues on. You created those moments that became memories, asking for nothing in return. So the question was, "Could I stand the rain? Because there will be stormy weather." I've endured and each storm has equipped me and made me a little stronger for the next. So I say thank you for the heads up Bobby.

# On My Mind

Thinking of you because you are all that is on my mind. This poem I'm writing is not meant to rhyme. It passed through my mind that two wrongs don't make a right. I mean we fuss and fuss but still you were right. You say you love me and I know that I love you, so let's cut to the chase and let our dreams come true.

Time after time it crossed my mind, how could love be in my face but still I was blind. I came into your life for three great reasons: to love, to respect, and to be treated even.

I guess you can say I was wrong for what happened in the past, but the past was yesterday. I just want what we had to last. So let's start over today, tomorrow, and forever. Can you stand the rain? Because there will be stormy weather.

# Scared Feelings

I try but I can't get inside your mind to find your scared feelings that are hidden inside.

It makes me wonder how do you really feel, keeping to yourself and not letting anyone in.

You say only what you want people to hear, that makes me wonder do you really care.

I try and open up to you to see if you would do the same.

So far no luck, you're still playing these old silly games.

I'm not going to give up, even though I've had no luck.

I'm going to keep trying to find out what's really on your mind

And try to make you let go of these scared feelings you keep inside.

Don't be ashamed to tell me how you feel, because I am going to always whisper my thoughts in your ear

# The cost of a friendship, the value of a friend

When talking about my two best friends of over twenty years, it brings me great joy to know that our relationship is real. Life has not always been rainbows in the sky, but no matter what obstacles may have come, or what circumstances we've encountered, our relationship has withstood the tests of time. Some may ask what is the cost of a friendship or the value of a friend. I would simply say the friendship didn't cost anything but having true best friends is priceless, so valuable that you cannot put a dollar amount on it. We each have our own struggles but for one of my friends, I tell her that the average person could not endure the struggles she's had and still manage to keep it all together. I admire her strength and I love her willingness to take on every challenge, no matter how hard or rigorous it may be. When you have been through a few storms in life, you learn really quickly that you will need someone there to help you regroup, refocus, and regain your motivation to continue on. Through the tears, the laughter, and growing pains, we have stood beside one another. If you look up trial and error in the imaginary dictionary, you will surely see our faces next to those words. We each lead different lives, have different personality types, and dance to the beat of our own drums. Nevertheless, we have so much in common and I know that I can count on them no matter how crazy life may get.

The importance of sharing my friendship is to say this: we all need someone to connect with. We had no idea back in 1993 when we were teenagers that our friendship would span over twenty years, but I'm so grateful that I had them along the way to lean on. I will be the first to tell you to guard your heart and to choose your friends wisely. But I will also be the first to tell you that you can't be so guarded that you don't feel a need to have a friend or a confidant that you can count on.

I have made some mistakes in befriending people who never had good intentions, and I had to learn how to discern and know who was for me and who was against me. Through it all, in spite of the fakes and counterfeits, I fared pretty well when it came to having real friends. The most important thing to know when it comes to building friendships or relationships is that you have to be willing to accept them as they are. Never try to change a person, but if there is something that they need to work on, allow them the time and space to do so on their own. Part of being in a friendship is to know all there is to know about the person, good, bad, or indifferent, and still be able to be in relationship with them.

I encourage you, if you don't have at least one person that you know you can trust, look within yourself and see if you are the reason why people don't hang around very long. Is that an area that has yet to be healed? Are there emotional wounds that the scab hasn't started to take form? I've pushed people away and out of my life for years, dismissing them before I ever gave them a chance. My unhealed emotions couldn't trust them and I kept them at bay. Immediately, they would label me as being mean and antisocial because they didn't know my story. They couldn't have known my pain; they just knew what was standing before them.

What I have learned is that you have to show yourself friendly in order to make friends. When I started to change my attitude and outlook about people, I found that there were a lot of loving, friendly people that were just like me, looking and searching for someone who shared common ground. We can get so caught up in our emotions that we lose our self in the commotion. We can become so broken that we end up causing more harm than good to the situation. Many of us struggle within ourselves because we have not yet learned what it is to be loved or how to reciprocate it. It is very important to know and understand what love really and truly is to be able to move forward in the healing process.

Normally you hear people tell others that they love them all the time. Husbands tell their wives and vice versa. Parents tell their children they love them, and children tell their parents and so on. It's common to speak those three touching words, but so often those words can become cliché and it becomes conditioned in us to say them without truly knowing what love is. Without love, we gain nothing. Without love, we lack the one thing that will help us forgive and receive our healing. I encourage you to start treating those wounds with love and watch how they start to heal. Don't allow your past pain to take root. Remember that if it does not take root, it cannot grow. We have all at some point in time been hurt or betrayed by others and in our emotional state, we wanted to repay hurt with hurt but end up hurting undeserving people that came along. As I look back throughout my life,

I would literally run people off. I would be so guarded and unwilling to trust anyone that they just figured it wasn't worth trying to get to know me through all those walls I had built up. It wasn't that they had done anything wrong, but I was too bruised and too sore to even give them a chance. I had harbored unforgiveness in my heart for so long that it became natural to me. Those doors of hurt from my past remained opened, keeping me looking back through it and being reminded of the hurt over and over again. It was because of those opened doors that I continued to suffer and kept those wounds open and exposed, unable to heal. Little did I know, help was on the way and those doors from my past would eventually be shut and walls were coming down.

If you find that unforgiveness has taken the place of love in your heart, it's not too late to start forgiving those who have hurt you. Hurt can be unexpected, unintentional but still damaging. I suffered major setbacks and stagnation as a result of that very thing. As I have come to know, you can stay in a dead situation far too long and instead of growing, you lose ground. The key is not to lose sight of where you are trying to go. Don't let unforgiveness isolate you from those who will offer comfort and support during those times.

# B.F.F

# (Best Friends Forever)

So you say I am your BFF, your ace boon Coon,

Well let's keep it real because that's what we do.

We be down with each other like four flat tires,

But wait a minute and let me see how I'm going to finish this rhyme.

Yes we have a friendship, and some may find it crazy that

We are so close we're like Fred Sanford and old shady Grady.

Nick knack paddy whack give a dog a bone,

Why can't I get my BFF to answer this phone?

So you say I am your BFF, your ace in the hole

That means I'll tell you when to pump your brakes and when to slow your

roll.

These three words sweet and simple, these three words will always kindle.

Nicely fitted together so what we have will stay intact

You know this friendship is real because we go way back.

# My Happiness

So you may ask where is my happiness. Is it in my smile, in a kiss, or maybe a
hug?
My happiness has yet to be discovered, so can you please show me some love.

My happiness! What does that mean, my happiness is undiscovered and yet
to be seen.
Is it in the pain I feel, or in the tears I'd cried? I laid my happiness to rest
because today it died.

Is my happiness words on a page, or a song we sang?
If my happiness is real, then why so much pain?

My happiness was as clear as the rainbow, as long as the sea is wide.
My happiness is being resurrected and it will come back alive.

A distant memory, another sad love song, still trying to figure out what went
wrong.
Don't get it twisted, happiness is great, it's a peace of mind topped with a big
smile on my face.

But isn't my happiness supposed to be within? Yes it is and, my happiness, I will see you again.

So you may ask where is my happiness. Is it in my smile, in a kiss, or maybe a hug?

No my happiness is me being me and a heart filled with love.

# The Fight of My Life

Hurting, crying, and confused from so much pain.

I need to free my mind before I go insane.

What is a battered woman to do?

I shield myself and I try to fight, but I'm still black and blue.

Love and trust is how a relationship should be based, not throwing fists into

each other's face.

Is it my fault? Why can't I just leave?

I'm so tired of being your punching bag, accusing me of some man named

Steve.

I don't know who he is. I promise I don't know.

I guess you didn't hear me; you were too busy knocking my head up against

this door.

I'm making my great escape; I'm running for my life, this is my only chance.

I'm giving it the best fight of my life.

# And let the church say Amen!

I want to share with you what caused my healing to have to start again as a result of being hurt within the church. It's not uncommon for people to be hurt by others but imagine the pain when it's from within the four walls of a church. Church should not leave you feeling like you just got robbed without a gun or that you just got condemned to hell just because you showed up to Sunday service. It's sad to say that some churches are being led by men and women with hidden agendas; they are stealing, killing, and destroying the people. They use false teachings to deceive you and to trick you into believing what they say is true and that their actions are real and you should go right along with it with no questions asked.

We can have blinders on when it comes to people in positions and with titles. We can begin to hold these individuals in such high regard that we make them superior and lose sight of what is really going on behind closed doors. We trust these people and because of this trust, we tend to let our guard down and just go with it, but we never get to a place where we stop them from hurting us emotionally.

There was this underlying control that kept me stuck in a rut and trying to measure up based on what other people thought of me. I found myself in bondage by allowing those I held in high regard because of their title or position to not only hold my past against me, dangling it over my head, but also to steal my joy. They had their way of controlling and manipulating through guilt and condemnation. As long as they kept me feeling as if I had done too much to be forgiven, I always looked to them as my saving grace. This fed into their egos and insecurities, but they always painted their lives to be picture perfect. No one is perfect!

Every decision made had to be screened and pre-approved. People had to be given the ok to proceed and if you didn't follow along, you were ostracized for making your own decisions when it came to you or your family. There is a big difference between getting guidance and counseling versus being controlled and told what you can and cannot do. There was discord, division, gossiping, spying, and cover-ups to say the least; all coming from those who carried those important titles. You were always being sized up by what designer name you wore or what kind of vehicle you drove, where you lived, where you worked, etc. If you sought counseling, your private issues would be a headline in that week's gossip column. If you dared question their motives, others were put on high alert and ordered not to associate with you anymore because you no longer had anything in common with them. It was indeed a modern day secret society – or better said a hidden cult amongst the "believers."

It had devastating consequences for those like me who bought into the deception but then came into the knowledge and truth of it all. There was this urgency to get out, but the guilt kept you there, returning week after week for more punishment. I became depressed and I isolated myself from others because those old wounds had become exposed again. I harbored unforgiveness and I was justified in my own eyes, because other people had created the hurt. I'm here to tell you from a place of restoration that it's not an excuse, so take back your healing. Don't misconstrue the message behind the story. This story doesn't apply to every church but these people and places do exist.

I share this with you because there were others who were hurt as a result of what was going on. I can say that all of them have not recovered from the experience and it's sad to see innocent, trusting people suffer emotionally because of others' selfish actions. I am sounding the alarm and if you find yourself in a similar situation, I encourage you to remove yourself without any shame or guilt. Trust that small still voice in your heart that says, "This is not right."

I want to encourage you to not give up because you are important to God and he loves you unconditionally. We have to begin to see ourselves the way God sees us, apart from our mistakes. Don't think that you are not good enough for His love because you are very special in His eyes. The love that God gives to me, He gives to everyone. Don't be misled; we are not to let other people continue to hurt us when we have identified that they are knowingly and willingly doing so. You love them but at the same time you don't open yourself up to more hurt, because it can produce resentment, bitterness, and strife within you that will stop you from healing.

The most important thing to take away from this story is that no matter who, what, when, or where the hurt originated from, we must forgive and love those who hurt us. It's ok if you have to start your healing again; the important thing is that you've started! I'm here to encourage you to keep striving and pushing your way through, moving forward to better and greater things in life.

# For All I Gave

For all that I gave was all that I had. I wish I'd known that there was a hole in this bag.

For all that I gave just fell right to the floor, so silly to think those sounds I should ignore.

But there you were, one step behind, taking what I gave, except you stole it this time.

The deception of it all to say the least, with your game plan in motion, you selfishly chased after me.

For all that I gave was all that I had. Can you please take this dagger out of my back?

Though I bled onto the floor, you can't kill me; superficial wounds are neither fatal nor deadly as you see.

I never knew how strong I was and since I don't fight with weapons, I'll just kill you with my love.

# Let Them Flow

You can't see the tears that fall down my face, because they only roll down when I'm alone and in my secret place.

I let them flow as to no end; I let them flow because they know all that I have hidden within.

Pour out of me; release yourself from the guilt and shame. Fall into this puddle that reveals the reflection and the innocents of this hurting face. One by one they all fall; these tears roll down to reveal the stories that go untold.

I felt them roll down the sides of my cheeks. I watched the path that each tear took; so warm as they fell onto the pages of this book.

Come with me, I'm not afraid. I trust you when you say sometimes it takes the hand of another to wipe those tears away.

I see a smile emerging from the tears, I hear laughter echoing through the air, feeling the rhythm of my life and all that it has to share.

Yes, please take me to this secret place that you speak so freely of. Take me to where all my tears flow in what I call the river of love.

# Misery

So much hurt so much rain, this everlasting feeling of endless pain.

No excuses, no reason why; all night long all I do is cry.

Over and over again, up and down, this roller coaster keeps going round and round.

Enough is enough, there can't be anymore, all of this unhappiness has to go.

New faces to see, new things to do. So long misery, you and I are through.

A new sense of peace and a stable state of mind, misery has packed up and I've said my goodbyes.

"Goodbye misery, so long," I said, "Tonight is the night I killed you dead."

# Focused

For so long the unknown was lurking outside my mind but unable to find its way in.

A bruised heart, an ego torn, your lips lied to me for far too long.

Now wounded, weary, and sad you have lost the love that you once had.

Focusing on a new beginning, you no longer exist because I have written a different ending.

No looking back into the past but straight ahead into life anew.

Now I can rejoice because I have finally gotten rid of you.

You are no more, so watch out! Don't get hit by that swinging door.

# The heart beats with such great strength...

Have you ever wanted something so badly, but the more you tried to attain it, the harder it became to grab hold of? Chasing after people or things that were never meant for you to have can create a false sense of failure. Believing that you have failed opens the door for disappointment, regret, resentment, and other emotions to creep in leaving you feeling defeated.

I often hear people talk about the mistakes they've made in their past, and I'm guilty of doing this as well, but were they all really mistakes? In the book of Exodus (KJV) chapter 14, the children of Israel thought that they had made a mistake by fleeing out of Egypt. Can you imagine how Moses must have felt when he knew he was being led by God? In verse twelve (KJV) it reads, " Is not this the word that we did tell thee in Egypt, saying, let us alone, that we may serve the Egyptians? For it had been better for us to serve the Egyptians, than that we should die in the wilderness." The children of Israel were being led out of slavery and captivity but when it seemed as though the situation took a turn for the worse, they actually suggested that it was better if they had just stayed in bondage rather than to be free. As the story continues, Pharaoh and his army were defeated and the Children of Israel continued their journey into the promise land.

In every relationship, you really have to evaluate how and why it all came to be. Really look at the people that make up these relationships and search for those things that connect you to them. You have to look beyond what your eyes can see and line your heart up with your mind and thoughts. Your heart may be telling you to approach the matter in one way, but your gut feeling tells you to go about it in another. Find the truth between the two and make the best decision for you at that time. You have to know what it is that you desire and want out of life. Knowing what you want keeps you from guessing who or what will make you happy. If it turns out that you should've gone with the latter choice, just regroup, refocus, and start again.

Learn from what that decision taught you, apply it, and move forward. Your goal is to be able to minimize the chances of having emotional setbacks. No one gets it right one hundred percent of the time; you have to start seeing the glass as half full instead of half empty. Although we may not always make the best decision, there is always a lesson to be learned when we realize we could have made a different choice and that there was always an alternate route. When it came to relationships, I will be the first to admit that I've yet to figure out this thing called love. What past relationships taught me was to tread lightly, guard my heart, and proceed with caution, but that approach has yet to yield me the results I desire. So I had to reevaluate and see what alternative routes were available for me, while still leading to the same destination. While on this journey, I discovered that you cannot be afraid to love and open up your heart to new people. Yes, there are those who have no clue whatsoever what it truly means to love unconditionally and without judgment, but then again we all have to learn what true love is and how to love others. You'll know that it's real when you can know all there is to know about a person, the good and the bad, and still be able to maintain that relationship because you can see beyond the outer appearance and see straight through to the very core of their heart.

Don't allow heartbreak to keep you for finding that which is real and genuine. Forgive those who broke your heart and don't compare new relationships to old ones. You have to guard your heart but only to the point where the bad can't infiltrate. I'm still learning how to accept things as they are versus how I may want them to be. If it's a relationship, treat it as such. If it's a friendship, build that foundation and stand firm on it without confusing the two. A relationship is only as strong as its foundation, so make it indestructible!

# Wait and See

I see your face when I close my eyes and think of how you graced me with your warm and captivating smile.

Those big brown eyes, I couldn't ignore, glaring at me as I passed you in a hurry, walking under the corridor.

The first encounter, our spirits agreed that you would be a great husband; I'm thinking one for me.

You complimented me; oh how sweet it was to hear such a pure and innocent voice.

You look beautiful today the voice said so effortlessly, how handsome he was looking back at me.

I let you get away, how could that be? Maybe the timing was off and you again I will see.

Who was this man that came out of nowhere? Who was this man that has reappeared into thin air?

So many years, I just couldn't believe and once again you slipped away from me.

Letting you get away, keeps me reliving that moment even now until this very day.

Will there be a third encounter, it just has to be. You, me in the same place; just you wait and see!

# ON THE LINE

Let's lay it all on the line; I have to let you go this time?

There is nothing easy about giving your love away. But I'll hold our memories close to my heart and that's where they will always stay.

There are no words to express what's really in my heart. There is no comfort for my tears as I lay here crying in the dark.

I gave it a lot of thought, I pondered it in my mind, the love I had for you was like fine wine that only got better with time.

I know your happiness, and I see glimpses of your pain. It's only when you smile that my heart ignites like a flame.

Two's company and three is a crowd, not sure where I fit in so I will graciously bow out.

Letting go is hard to do because I will just keep right on thinking of you.

So let's lay it all on the line; I have to let you go this time?

# Falling In Love With You

Guarding my heart because that's all I know to do.
 Shielding and protecting it because I made a mistake by falling in love with
you.
Keeping my distance; uncertain what that means....
This is the worst case of heartbreak I've ever seen.

Grabbing hold to all that I know to do;
Yes, it's time that I let go of you.
I don't understand.... You say you love me so.
 I guess love wasn't enough for your heart to want me even more.

Guarding my heart because that's all I know to do.
Shielding and protecting it because I made a mistake by falling in love with
you.

# A Piece of His Heart

How do you mend a heart that's not broken? Or dry tears from eyes that can't cry? Having this overwhelming feeling of being in love with a guy.

I know that he loves me, it's been that way from the very start, but I can't have all of him, he says just a piece of his heart.

How do you mend a heart that's not broken? Or dry tears from eyes that can't cry? Always hiding my feelings within and each day I keep asking myself why?

Because I want to have all of you puts my heart and mind at war. Asking myself where do I go from here as I keep walking through this revolving door. The mind is strong and the heart beats with such great strength, but how long will this go on and can I really handle this?

You have me tucked securely in your heart, but what does that really mean? If you let go and walked away, can my heart truly be set free? Free to love, free to give, and free to find someone who wants me their heart to give.

So how do you mend a heart that's not broken? Or dry tears from eyes that can't cry? Figure out a way to get over being in love with this guy.

# I'm in love

I'm in love with a man; I'm in love.
Charting dangerous waters, unsure what's lurking ahead.
Watch out for trouble, this voice keeps telling me in my head.

I'm in love with a man; I'm in love.
Just being in your presence makes me all warm inside
Being held close in your arms creates a smile that I just can't hide.

I'm in love with a man, I'm in love.
I've been here before, can I trust what I feel,
I need to know from you if loving me is for real.

I'm in love with a man, I'm in love.
How do you explain, how do you put it all into words?
Maybe you can write me a song that no one has ever heard.

I'm in love with a man, I'm in love.
Make it special; write it just for me,
Whisper it in my ear so our love can be set free.
I'm in love with a man, but is that man in love with me?

# Why are you pushing me away?

I believe that, without a shadow of a doubt, some people are purposefully sent to be a part of our lives. We may not initially know why they have become a part of our lives or how long they will be around but they are there for a reason. Several years ago, I had that person show up and honestly, I had no clue how important of a role he would play. As the months turned into years, the picture started to become clear that he was not going anywhere. After many years of friendship, I now know that he held several keys that were used to lock doors that kept a negative past looking into my future. He came into my life during the time when I had not started my healing, as a matter of fact; I had not even realized that I needed healing. I was very cautious of him because it seemed as though he just popped up out of nowhere. Who was this guy and why was he so interested in getting to know me? I was not going to be this naive little girl who was going to be taken advantage of by this older guy. I was smarter than that.

It is so funny now looking back and seeing how much of a hard time I gave him, but he continued to stick by my side. We developed a friendship that has now spanned over a decade and he is one of my best friends. If I've ever met a man so genuine and loving, it would be this guy. As long as I have known him, he has been consistent with being a caring and compassionate gentleman, always putting others before himself. If he could tell his story, I'm sure he would say that dealing with me was not always easy and I'm sure there were times when he wanted to just walk away. He has repeatedly asked me throughout the years, "Why are you pushing me away?" I would always jokingly say, "Apparently I haven't pushed hard enough because you are still here."

I never saw my actions as pushing him away, but as me running away out of fear of him hurting me. I had not trusted anyone for a long time and out of nowhere he pops into my life and I'm just supposed to let my guard down and trust him. That was not going to happen.

Surely this man had a hidden agenda and I was not going to be suckered into thinking he was doing all of this just because he saw something greater on inside of me that I couldn't see within myself. Well, I can now say that I was wrong and after all of these years he has not changed and he has yet to ask anything of me other than to be the friend to him as he is to me.

What I had not realized during the early stages of our friendship was that I couldn't trust the way he treated me. I couldn't understand why this man who seemingly wanted nothing from me would just keep coming around. He was always encouraging and attentive when I had issues that I wanted to talk with him about. He was never judgmental or critical of the things I shared with him but he would be truthful and would tell me if he thought my actions were wrong. I often look back and think how in the world did he put up with me all of these years? I'm sure he would tell you that I have said and done things that made him question why he even bothered trying to get to know me. There have been a few instances where he would just take a step back, give me my space, and watch from a very short distance. I came to realize that no matter how many times I ran away from him or how hard I pushed, he was not going anywhere or at least going very far.

He has always stood firm and he stood tall, he was unmovable. I can truly say that he helped me tear down walls of hurt, mistrust, deception, unforgiveness, and anger. I wouldn't have understood what love really was if he had just spoken the words, but because he exemplified it, it made all the difference. Not to say that he didn't have things going on in his life where he may have needed me to be there for him, but he was undeterred and he would always say, "Such is life; you just have to keep moving".

My friend didn't knock down any walls for me, neither did he close any doors; he simply held my hand and walked with me through that phase of my life. He would only push when I was ready no matter how long it took, and he was careful not to push until after I started. Having him by my side made it easier and less scary to face what was stopping my healing. Had he taken any other approach, the story would have been very different, but because of his love, patience, and endurance, I can now be the friend to him that he has always been to me.

Now, if I were reading this story as if it belonged to someone else, my first thought would be, He sounds like a great guy, why not a relationship beyond a friendship? My response would simply be that our purpose was to be a real friend when the other one needed it most. Life will knock you down, but it is always easier getting up when you have a helping hand extended to you.

If I could give you a peek inside of his heart, you would see these words: "Sometimes life moves us along so quickly that it's not always easy to find something real and lasting to hold on to. In the midst of this busy world, I take comfort in the true steadfast gift of our friendship."

The journey has not always been easy, but when you work hard at something, you will do that much more to make sure it's even harder to lose. We have worked hard at keeping our friendship intact and making it work through the toughest of times.

# For Always

No matter how far you are or where you may be,
For Always
Our hearts will systematically beat.

We stand together, we stand tall
For Always
Two pillars in this world that cannot fall.

I got you and you got me,
For Always
We are stronger together rooted and grounded like a tree

My Care Bear, My Tender Heart,
For Always
You have been down with me from the start.

You gave me a reason, you gave me a song
For Always
A smile on my face as I write this poem.

Ten years in the making, this love becomes real,

For Always

A friend of mine and the deal has been sealed.

# Rock with Me

So you want to rock with me but you say I'm just a friend.
Rocking with me means you take me as I am and not play with my emotions.

You want to rock with me, then come and take me by the hand.
Uncover the mysteries of the mind and see that I'm not the average woman.

Poetically and rhythmically my words flow from deep within
From the darkness of this prison in my mind that has given me a life
sentence.

So you want to rock with me, you have to see past these walls
Look into the realms of my heart; is it worth you really getting involved?

Oh yes, now I remember there is more work that needs to be done,
So love me in a special way and your prize, my heart, you have won.

# Can You Hear the Music

I have great expectation, endless possibilities and such determination.

The view from here excites me from within; if no one else will do it, I know that I can.

Patiently waiting and eagerly anticipating the next move. This life of mine dances to the beat of a different tune.

Can you hear the music? Do you know the song? I've put it on repeat so I can dance all night long to the beat of my own drum.

Love Is Tangible or Emotional?

## Sunrise

I woke up this morning just in time to see the sun rise. How beautiful she was as the light broke through right before my eyes.

So calm and graceful as she rose into her place, closing my eyes and imagining you there, kissing me gently on my face.

"Good morning, beautiful," I could hear you say so soft and sweet. A good morning it was, but then I realized there was no one there but me.

# Rescue Me

Rescue me, save me, shield and protect.

Love me, hug me and never forget.

Tell me and show me;

 Make it crystal clear how much you care for me,

 And that you will always be there.

Trust me, know me and hear what I say.

Comfort me and hold me just like you did on yesterday.

Talk to me, look at me and see that it's real.

Laugh with me but don't cry for me, just wipe away my tears.

# UPON MY FACE

A gentle touch, a heartfelt embrace; the softness of your lips pressing on my face.

Your smile, your laugh, kisses on my head says more than any words that can ever be said.

We share our secrets, our inner most thoughts, so close to my heart, yes you are my rock.

You know so much about me, even the words unsaid, still loving your kisses on my head.

I'm so grateful for every moment that we share and those love songs that you whisper in my ear.

You take me to places I've never seen before, not wanting it to end, longing for more and more.

I get lost in the depths of your eyes, wondering what memories you hold inside.

As I pull you in and closer to me, a feeling so sweet as I hear the rhythm of
your heartbeat.

A gentle touch, a heartfelt embrace; the softness of your lips pressing on my
face.

# That Girl

Am I that girl you dream about?
Am I that girl who keeps you in deep thought?
Is it me who you fantasize of holding in a warm embrace?
Is it me you desire to passionately kiss you on your face?

Warm, caring, compassionate, and kind;
That's me, that girl who stays on your mind.

Yes it's me tugging at your heart and stirring up your emotions.
Do you wonder if it's time to put your love into motion?

Am I that girl who sets your heart ablaze?
Am I that girl who encourages you day by day?
Who me? Yes me! If not me, then who?
Beautiful, smart, and definitely one of a kind.

I am that girl who makes you say, ''I want that girl to be mine!

# Ten

When I first saw you, I was scared to talk to you. After I got to know you I was scared to open up to you. When you became my friend, I was scared to love you. Now that I love you, I am scared to lose you.

Ain't love funny, comical you might say; I didn't see this one coming, how my love just up and went away. Random thoughts, unfocused mind, there was no winning for me this time.

I never thought that falling in love could be so rough, but having to say goodbye has been very tough. I wanted to be the reason why you chose to stay; I wanted to be the reason that smiles come to your face.

Do I keep loving you or do I let go? Do I hold on tight and give it the best fight of my life? Do I graciously bow out, and wave the white flag, surrender my love and all that we had?

You and me, me and you, the both of us together made an awesome two. I'll love you from a distance, I'll love you from afar, and I'll miss you dearly, because you hold the keys to my heart.

No tears to shed and no love lost, ten years of memories I'll always hold in my heart. I'm letting go of all of my fears, and I'm thinking why not just count down another ten years.

## Someone to Love

I'm looking for someone to love me and someone for me to love. I have found the task to be trying and a challenge that I did not expect, but I know that he is out there waiting to be met.

He is so charming; I can't believe that I'm actually glowing. Look at that smile, how beautifully it spreads across his face, making his gleaming eyes squint as I stare into his face.

His love shines so bright, his words are so pure; his laugh pierces through me like a raging bull. How powerful is his touch and look how smooth he is with his strut. He makes me shine from within, I'm asking myself, could it be that he is that man?

Is he that someone for me to love? Is he someone who will love me? The mysteries of the heart so nicely tucked away. I can feel the rhythm when our bodies are closely embraced.

Could it be that he is that someone who will truly love me? The one who will lock up my heart and never throw away the key?

# Love and Happiness

I can still remember the first time we met, that special day I'll never forget. When I saw you I was really surprised, I couldn't believe it when I looked into your eyes.

There was this feeling deep inside my heart that we'll always be together and never apart. When you said you loved me just as I love you, it first seemed impossible, but I guess that is up to you.

Trust me with your heart and I'll trust you with mine. Together we will become one and freeze ourselves in time. So let's make this official and seal it with a kiss, you and me together equals true love and happiness.

# I Didn't Always Get It Right

My plan was simple, thought out so well that nothing about it could go wrong. I had purposed in my heart that there would be no sex before marriage and after four years of celibacy and no meaningful relationship in sight, being single and saved had some valuable lessons to teach me.

I would like to tell you that "it just happened" but the truth of the matter was, my flesh was weak and had been for several months. It started with just a thought in my mind, but when I failed to cast down those imaginations I allowed it to take root. Over the next several months, the urges and desires became more intense and more frequent. Unfortunately, I have to say that I never made it to the fifth year of celibacy. It would be a typical response to say "the devil made me do it" but it was up to me to take the way of escape provided, but I didn't. I knew my actions were wrong and in my heart, I really wanted to stop, but I had given too much control to my flesh at that point to just stop. It took some well thought out tactics of the devil to get me to that place, and now it was going to take an even more thought out plan of attack to defeat the enemy.

I have been to countless single's meetings, single's retreats, and single's revivals but what it failed to teach me was how to be single and saved. No one talked about the temptations of being single; at least not at any of the one's I attended or was a part of. Even though we were all adults trying to walk the walk, no one was talking the talk. We were all just left out there to fend for ourselves. But what I needed to know was what did you do when faced with sexual temptation? How did you overcome the lust and desires? The truth of the matter was, everyone wanted to have this picture perfect walk with Jesus with no obstacles, no temptations and no valley's to climb out of, but we know that is not true.

Everyone's struggles are not the same, but if your struggles are the same as mine, tell me what did you do? To get those answers I had to come face-to-face with the reality of my situation. I was living under a cloud of condemnation and didn't know how to get out from under its downpours. Living with the guilt left me feeling weak and lost, but then I realized that it was an illusion. As a result of trying to "fix me" the funny thing was, I would keep waking up with those same temptations staring me in the face.

Surely I must have missed a step somewhere along the way. I must have done something wrong or forgotten something. In James 5:16 (KJV) it tells us to confess our faults one to another and pray one for another. Now let me tell you something about myself. I am one of those believers who believes that God has a sense of humor, but surely He didn't mean that I should literally go and tell those judgmental, hypocritical, rock throwers my business? I have been in church for a long time and one thing I know for sure is that most of them carry around a bag of rocks on their backs, ready to stone you to death on site for any confession of sin or wrong doing.

Well guess what, they won't get me. I refuse to be a sitting target for those who want you to believe that they are perfect and that they can do no wrong. I know this because I use to be one of those people and it became very clear to me that the very thing that I feared the most is what I had done to others. I had judged them!

There is a difference between conviction and condemnation. We are convicted when we have done something wrong, but the conviction is only to alert us that we need to get back on track. On the other hand, condemnation comes to destroy you, tear you down, and make you feel unworthy. Condemnation keeps you reliving the situation and keeps you bound by your past mistakes. Then there is self-condemnation when you beat yourself up to the point that you feel as if there is no turning back. Then there is the condemnation from those stone throwers, those people who lie in wait for an opportunity to stone you to death.

God tells us numerous times to leave the past behind. Why would He tell us to leave the past behind if it was not crucial to our future? If it were not possible for Him to erase our past, He wouldn't keep reminding us to leave it there. What I have come to realize is that I had yet to fully grasp how much God loves me and that my faults didn't make Him love me any less. I had to ask for forgiveness for all of those people I judged and I then asked for forgiveness for judging myself and holding myself captive.

If the truth sets you free, then it would be safe to say that a lie will keep you in bondage. Although I felt compelled to confess my faults to some ladies that I had been in a prayer group with, the grip of fear was very tight. There were always new faces, some stayed and others just passed through. They all seemed so loving and compassionate about their spiritual walk but the fear inside of me said not to confide in these ladies. But this particular night, I couldn't shake the feeling of confessing what I had done. I just knew from past experiences that they would judge me and probably kick me out of the prayer group. I needed that prayer group; I needed to be in an environment that kept me connected to my faith.

My mind was made up; I was keeping my mouth shut! Would you believe that the more I fought against it, the more urgency came over me to spill the beans? In my silence came a river of tears as I battled in my mind what to do. Some of the ladies took notice and inquired, but since I was being mute about the matter, they decided that they would not press the issue but they asked if I would let them pray for me. I agreed and the more they prayed the more those dreadful words bubbled to the surface. "I've sinned, I have fornicated."

One of the ladies looked me square in the face and said, "Is that it? I thought you had killed somebody the way you were carrying on. Honey we have all been through this but don't let it get you down." One by one, the other ladies started to encourage me and spoke heartfelt words of love. It was at that moment that I realized that in spite of my fear, none of those women judged me. The release of guilt immediately left as this warmth of love poured out on me. 1 Peter 4:8 (NIV) reads, "Above all, love each other deeply, because love covers over a multitude of sins." I was now free from the guilt and shame because their love covered my sin.

Don't sacrifice your future because of your past. You have to be able to accept the things you cannot change and get back up more times than you are knocked down. Getting beyond judgment is realizing that our imperfections do not define who we are, but show us that we can overcome where we've been.

You have to decide that you will neither dodge stone throwers, nor throw stones in retaliation. Every time a stone or accusation is thrown my way, I stand and allow God to shield me from the impact. Those who know us the best and love us the most could point out our every fault, sin, and failure ... but those who love never cast stones.

# Agony of Defeat

As I lay here in your arms so big and so strong, holding me safe and secure all night long.

As we lay, I could hear the songwriter say all of me loving all of you as our two hearts became one beat instead of two.

As I rest my head on your chest, and I gaze into your eyes knowing soon it will be time for you to say goodbye.

Walking you to the door, there comes this agony of defeat, but I know there is a hug and a kiss for me.

I don't want you to go but what can I do? I have no answers; I just know that my heart loves you.

# What I Believe

When it's all said and done, tell me what you see.

I see perfect skies and beautiful rainbows, the promise that you made to me.

I see tomorrow on the horizon, I see the rising of the sun.

Having no worries of what the day may bring because the battle is already

won.

Promises of love cascading through the air;

Reach up and grab it but you have to handle it with care.

Give a little then share a lot; it's more than enough.

Trust him when he says to you, we are more than a conqueror.

When it's all said and done, tell me what you see.

I see myself loving others through my hurt because that's what I believe.

# This Tree Has No Shade

As I stretched out under the sun taking in the rays, enjoying these blue skies because this tree has no shade.

Floating on air passing with ease, if you looked up these blue skies are what you would see.

The colors of my imagination are so vivid so clear, the whistling of the wind floating past my ear.

Enjoying the blue skies, watching heaven stand still, the colors of my imagination seeing angels appear.

So peaceful, so serene all of my cares just float away; come go with me and let's just enjoy one another on this sunny and beautiful day.

Look at the footprints see what the clouds have made. There is no better view than from under this tree that has no shade.

Living a poetic life, a smile from ear to ear, capturing every thought just as the sun reappeared.

As I stretched out under the sun taking in the rays, enjoying these blue skies because this tree has no shade.

# When It's Really Love...

I have shared my heart and expressed many variations of love, but now I present to you my one true love. The love that will never break my heart, never lie to me, neither deceive me, harm me, or leave me. This love is real and after many years of searching and finding false impressions, illusions, and imitations, I now know that it's really love.

I have searched for this love in smiles, in tears cried, hugs, kisses, gentle touches, warm embraces, gifts, and so on but to no avail. I sought out love in all the wrong places and as a result, I ended up on a wild goose chase. You have to make sure your time and efforts are being applied to that which is real.

Through it all, I have come to know that 4 Love suffers long and is kind; love does not envy; love does not parade itself, is not puffed up; 5 does not behave rudely, does not seek its own, is not provoked, thinks no evil; 6 does not rejoice in iniquity, but rejoices in the truth; 7 bears all things, believes all things, hopes all things, endures all things. 8 Love never fails. 1corinthians 13:4-8 (KJV)

I had to learn that the grass was not greener on the other side, but only greener where I watered it. I also learned that no matter which side was greener, both sides still needed to be cut. Whenever I planted seeds but failed to provide the essentials needed for it to grow and produce the expected outcome, I was left with nothing, meaning I wasted valuable time and resources in seeds that I was ill-equipped to care for. I'd failed to put enough time and effort into my investment to see a return.

Nevertheless, I got to this place where Love was pure, genuine and in its rarest form and I want to introduce to you no greater Love....

# No Greater Love

There is no greater love than for a man to give his all for me.

There is no greater love than for a man to hold and comfort me.

There is no greater love than for a man to lay down his life for me.

There is no greater love than for a man to guide and protect me,

There is no greater love than for a man to hold my life securely in his hands.

There is no greater love than Jesus, yes he is that man.

# The Key

I closed the door upon my heart and wouldn't let anyone in. I trusted and loved only to be hurt again.

I locked the door and threw away the key as hard and as far away as I could. Can I trust you? I'm thinking maybe I should.

You came into my life and made me change my mind. Just when I thought that the tiny key was lost forever and too hard to find.

You held out your hand and there I could see that nothing was impossible because you were holding that tiny little key.

# A Beautiful Thing

I remember the first time you made me smile,
You told a joke that kept me laughing for a while.

You could see it in my eyes, the joy that you bring.
Happiness on the inside of me is a beautiful thing.

You understood exactly all the things I'd been through.
You gave me a warm embrace and said, "I will always love you".

You tore down those walls and broke through my pain.
Happiness on the inside of me is a beautiful thing.

You were not afraid to show me your heart and all that is within,
I gave you mine, and the broken pieces you put back together again.

You ignited a fire that turned a flicker into a flame.
Happiness on the inside of me is a beautiful thing.

I've shared with you my quest of seeking love, and I have shared my pain of losing love, but also the happiness as I waited on love. We each have a story and a journey that must be traveled to get to that place called "there." My story may not be your story, but somewhere along the way, we have transitioned from one place to another, coping, managing, or adjusting to life's rollercoaster.

When it's all said and done, Love still remains. We have to stay in that place of always learning to love again and again and again. This has not been easy; truthfully it has been downright scary. However, my journey continues and I will keep going forward and if I have to start again, so be it.
Suppressing your feelings can keep you from the truth and keep you bound to a hurtful and painful past.

Avoid going back at all cost, and know what triggers the old you. Never get caught off guard and get thrown back to a hurtful place. Deal with it no matter how difficult it may be. It is better for you to deal with it than for it to deal with you.

Please follow me on Facebook at www.facebook.com/tangilaroberson

www.ingramcontent.com/pod-product-compliance
Lightning Source LLC
Chambersburg PA
CBHW022030090426
42739CB00006BA/361

*9 7 8 0 6 9 2 4 6 8 0 3 6 *